THE BATTLE OF THE ALAMO

👆 It was early morning when Santa Anna's army scaled the walls of the Alamo, engaging in the hand-to-hand combat that would lead to their victory. Though the Alamo defenders were outnumbered, they fought bravely.

THE AMERICAN WEST

THE BATTLE OF THE ALAMO

MIKE WILSON

MASON CREST PUBLISHERS

976.403
Wilson

Mason Crest Publishers
370 Reed Road
Broomall PA 19008

Copyright © 2003 by Mason Crest Publishers.
All rights reserved. Printed and bound in the
Hashemite Kingdom of Jordan.

First printing

1 3 5 7 9 8 6 4 2

Library of Congress Cataloging-in-Publication Data
on file at the Library of Congress

ISBN 1-59084-062-3

CONTENTS

The Alamo is one of the most recognizable landmarks of the American Southwest. The building was designated a National Historic Landmark in 1960.

1

THE SILENT GUNS

BY MARCH 5, 1836, THE TEXANS HAD BEEN TRAPPED INSIDE THE ALAMO for 12 days. William Travis, commander of the men inside the fort, had sent messages asking for help. The fewer than 200 men inside the Alamo were surrounded by more than 10 times that number of Mexicans.

There were brave men inside the Alamo. Davy Crockett, a former congressman, was one of the most famous Americans of the time. This frontiersman had traveled to Texas seeking adventure and stayed at the Alamo to help fight for the cause of Texas independence.

Jim Bowie was inside the Alamo as well, and Bowie, too, was famous. He carried with him at all times a large hunting knife that people called a "bowie" knife. He was respected for his bravery, but now Bowie had taken ill. In fact, he was too sick to even rise from his bed. He would be of little use in the fight against the Mexicans.

7

The first Bowie knife was made by Jim Bowie's brother, Rezin Bowie. It was one and a half inches wide and nine inches long. This was the knife that Jim Bowie wore the rest of his life. As Bowie became famous, others wanted to own a knife like Bowie's, and the knives were manufactured.

Most of the men inside the Alamo were Anglos—white inhabitants of North America who were not of Hispanic descent—but there also were some native Texans, or *Tejanos*. These men, descended from Spanish settlers and Native Americans, had joined the fight for the freedom of Texas.

The Mexicans bombarded the Alamo with cannons at night, keeping the Texans busy with **skirmishes** so that they could not rest. After 12 days of this, the Texans' nerves were shot. They had not lost a man during the **siege**—at least not yet. But Travis knew that the Mexicans hadn't really made an all-out assault. He also knew that there simply were too few Texans against too many Mexicans. The Texans also were in short supply of gunpowder. There were cannons in the Alamo, but not enough men to operate them properly. Death was almost certain—unless the reinforcements arrived.

Then, suddenly, in the middle of the afternoon on March 5, 1836, the Mexican guns grew silent. The Texans weren't firing their weapons, either. They needed to conserve ammunition to defend against the full-scale attack they knew must be

Jim Bowie, who led a colorful life as a smuggler and soldier, was born in the spring of 1796 in Kentucky. He spent all of his early life on the western frontier, as his family moved to Missouri and then to Louisiana.

By the time he was 19, Bowie was on his own. He bought land, hunted, and became involved in smuggling slaves. He loved adventure and good company, but he had a quick temper. Once during a knife fight he was cut in the hand. Because of this, he had a large, double-edged butcher knife made with a special guard over the handle. It was this knife that made Bowie famous.

On September 19, 1827, Jim Bowie got into a fight with several men. Although Bowie was shot several times, he managed to kill two men with his knife and drove off the rest. The fight was reported in national papers, making Bowie famous. The Bowie knife soon became a popular weapon; many of the men at the Alamo were wearing them when he arrived at the fort in 1836.

Bowie left Louisiana for Texas when he got in trouble with the government over a land deal. In 1831 he married the daughter of an important Texas ranch owner, became a Mexican citizen, and settled down in San Antonio. He spent time looking for gold mines and fighting Indians and Mexicans. His wife and father-in-law died from cholera, a deadly disease, in 1833.

In 1835 Bowie joined Stephen Austin's volunteer army. By the end of 1835 he was leading them in important battles against the Mexican army. Sam Houston sent Bowie to the Alamo with orders to destroy the fort and withdraw the troops. However, Bowie did not carry out this order. He believed that the fort could be defended, and that the Texans could stop the Mexicans in San Antonio.

James Bowie was a well-known fighter. After injuring himself on his own blade in a knife fight, he invented the Bowie knife, which is still used today.

coming. The question was, would reinforcements arrive before that attack occurred?

It was a cold spring day. The Texans huddled at their posts, trying to find shelter from the stiff north winds. As it grew dark, the exhausted Texans, chilled to the bone, tried to stay awake, tried to stay warm, and waited.

That night, it was quiet. For the first time in nearly two weeks, the Texans would have a chance to rest. Three sentries were posted on the walls of the fort to watch for a Mexican attack. Another man inside the fort remained awake to watch the fires.

There are two theories about how the Alamo got its name. One theory is that it was named after a Spanish officer of the same name who kept his troop there. The other theory is that it is named after the cottonwood trees that grow in that area. The Spanish word for cottonwood trees is *alamo*.

But while the Texans slept, the Mexican army was moving. By 11 o'clock that evening Mexican soldiers, **cavalry**, and cannons had been placed around the Alamo in position to attack. Mexican soldiers lay on their bellies on the cold, frozen ground and waited for the signal.

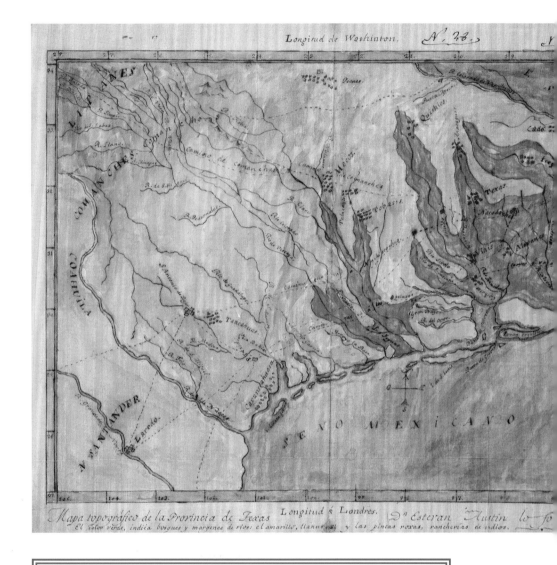

🖐 Stephen Austin created this map of the province of Texas in 1822, while he and his father were settling the land. The map was drawn on cloth and labeled in Spanish, and illustrates where the Americans settled in the eastern part of Texas.

TEXAS AND MEXICO

THE COUNTRY NOW CALLED MEXICO WAS ONCE RULED BY SPAIN. HERNANDO CORTÉS, THE Spanish **conquistador,** had conquered Mexico in 1519. By the 19th century, a small group of Spaniards controlled the top levels of government in Mexico. Below them in rank and power were Spaniards that had been born in Mexico called *criollos.* They owned a lot of the land and controlled **commerce**. Still further below them were a large group of persons of mixed blood, part Spanish and part Indian, called *mestizos.* At the very bottom, with the least power and respect, were the Indians that the Spanish had conquered. Although the society was divided up into these groups, the three lower groups all hated the very top group, the Spaniards from Europe. The Mexicans decided to revolt.

From about 1810 to 1821, the Mexicans fought their Spanish rulers for independence. However, after the Mexicans received their freedom, the fighting didn't stop.

The *criollos,* who controlled most of the land and commerce, wanted to rule the other groups pretty much as the Spaniards had. However, the *mestizos* and Indians wanted

The Mexicans originally had encouraged settlement of Texas by Anglo-Americans, approving 30 contracts to permit colonization. These were called "empresario" contracts. Anglos also were given temporary tax exemptions. One condition of an empresario contract was that the Anglo settlers had to become Catholics, because Catholicism was the state religion of Mexico.

the right to vote; they also wanted **civil rights**, separation of church and state, and other changes that didn't suit the *criollos* at the top. The Mexicans broke up into **factions** and fought with each other.

In addition, to the north in the province of Texas, Americans were arriving and forming settlements. They did not want to be ruled from Mexico City. In other parts of Mexico, there were groups that wanted freedom from a central Mexican government as well. These were called "Federalists." The more **conservative** group that wanted a strong central government and not much change in the social structure was called the "Centralists."

Although Texas was a Mexican province, Anglo-Americans had started moving there in the push westward. During the time that Spain ruled Mexico, an Anglo-American named Moses Austin had received permission to settle 300 families on 200,000 acres of territory. However, he died before he had a chance to establish the colony. His son, Stephen F. Austin, brought the Anglo settlers to Texas in January of 1822.

Stephen Fuller Austin is known as "the Father of Texas." He was born in Virginia and educated at schools in Connecticut and Kentucky. In 1821 he and his father, Moses Austin, went to Texas—then part of Spanish Mexico—intending to establish an American settlement there. After Moses died, Stephen continued with their plan. The 300 families who went with Stephen settled on the Colorado and Brazos rivers.

After Mexico won its independence, Austin acted as a go-between for the colonists and the Mexican government. In 1833, however, he was thrown in jail for 18 months.

When the Texas Revolution broke out, Austin was one of the leaders. He also went to Washington, D.C., to ask the U.S. government for help. He wanted the United States to make Texas part of its territories. He also gave many speeches to encourage people to support the cause of the Texans.

When the War for Texas Independence ended, Stephen F. Austin was named the Texas Republic's first secretary of state. However, he died soon after taking office, on December 27, 1836. Nine years later, as Austin had hoped, Texas officially became a U.S. state. The capital of the state of Texas, Austin, is named after him.

However, Mexico now was independent, and the new rulers objected to Austin's plans. Austin went to Mexico City and obtained permission again. Then he established the first colony of Anglo-Americans in Texas.

Over time, the increase in the number of Americans coming into Texas bothered the Mexicans. They passed a law in 1830 to prevent more Americans from settling there, but

Stephen F. Austin helped to colonize Texas, which became an independent republic and later, a part of the United States. He served as Secretary of State of the Republic of Texas during the last year of his life, 1836.

Austin found a way around the law, and the number of Americans continued to grow. Soon there were more Anglo-Americans in Texas than there were Mexican Texans. And the hostility between the Mexican rulers and the American colonialists continued to grow.

Stephen Austin tried to work with the Mexican government. Though the Mexicans had abolished slavery in 1824, Austin got the Mexicans to make an exception for the slave-owning Anglos in Texas. In 1833, Stephen Austin went to Mexico City to ask that Texas be allowed to form its own state government, while remaining a part of Mexico. Other Mexicans in Texas also wanted this, because state government would allow them to pass laws giving them more freedom.

Eventually, the Mexicans removed the law that prevented

more Americans from coming to Texas, but the government still did not let Texas form its own state government. On his way home from Mexico City, Austin was arrested and thrown in prison on suspicion of leading a rebellion. Austin was released from prison in July of 1835 and returned to Texas. However, the fact that Mexico had jailed Austin made many Anglos believe that war with Mexico was inevitable.

Mexico had adopted a **constitution** in 1824 that allowed each separate province or state in Mexico to have its own legislature and make laws. Now, with so much unrest in the country, the *criollos* were wondering if the 1824 constitution was a mistake. They were looking for a strong leader to restore

☞ Calling himself the "Napoleon of the West," Antonio López de Santa Anna was a formidable military leader. By the 1830s, he was Mexico's dictator.

order. In 1834, a military leader named Antonio López de Santa Anna overthrew the President of Mexico, dissolved the Congress of Mexico, and denounced the constitution of 1824. Mexico had become a dictatorship.

Under Santa Anna's rule, officers in any of the state governments could be dismissed whenever the central government liked. The state governments no longer had their own legislatures, and the **militias** raised by each state were reduced. This decreased the danger that a state could become strong enough to rebel against the central government.

Many states were unhappy with Santa Anna and said so. Finally, in 1835, two provinces of Mexico rebelled—Zapatecas and Texas.

Zapatecas had the largest state militia of any of the provinces—nearly 20,000 men who could be called on to fight and 4,000 already armed and ready to fight. They denounced the actions that Santa Anna had taken. On March 30, 1835, the legislature in Zapatecas passed a resolution authorizing the Zapatecas militia to resist troops from the central government of Mexico. They soon would have to do so.

The residents of Texas also rebelled. There was a big difference between Texas and Zapatecas, however. Although both regions wanted freedom from the Mexican government, the culture in Texas was different because the population was mostly Anglo.

On October 1, 1835, at a town called Gonzales, about 50

Antonio López de Santa Anna was a *criollo*, tall and muscular. Born on February 21, 1794, he joined the Spanish army when he was 16. He was very ambitious. By the time he was 18, he had been promoted to lieutenant. When he was 22, he became a captain.

Santa Anna was willing to do whatever he had to in order to get more power. In 1821, as Mexicans were fighting for their independence, Santa Anna was in charge of Spanish forces defending the city of Orizaba. However, he switched sides and helped the rebels defeat the Spanish army.

When Spain gave Mexico its freedom, Santa Anna became a powerful leader in Mexico's military. He used the army to overthrow Agustin de Iturbide, who had declared himself emperor. Mexico then instituted a democratic form of government, and Santa Anna was elected president in 1831.

However, Santa Anna's policies became more repressive. By 1835, the government had become a dictatorship. He was determined to crush the rebellion of the Texans, and led a large army to the Alamo in the early spring of 1836.

After the battle of the Alamo, Santa Anna's army was crushed at the battle of San Jacinto. Defeated and disgraced, Santa Anna nonetheless kept control of Mexico for many years, until he was driven from office by reformer Benito Juárez. He died in 1876.

miles east of San Antonio, Texans refused to let Mexican soldiers take back a cannon that had been loaned to the town so it could defend itself from Indian attacks. In fact, the Texans fired the cannon at the Mexican army. Two Mexicans were killed in the fight that followed. This event was the beginning of the Texas Revolution.

Volunteers formed an army. On October 10, 1835, they captured 50 Mexican soldiers in a surprise attack at La Haia. The next day, they elected Stephen Austin to be their commander. Then they headed for San Antonio.

Santa Anna sent 1,200 Mexican troops to San Antonio de Bexar, as it was called then. Their leader was General Perfecto de Cós, the brother-in-law of Santa Anna. A small group of Texas volunteers fought with the Mexicans throughout October and November. When Austin left in November to seek help from the U.S. government, Edward Burleson took over as commander. However, the Texans were unable to take San Antonio and were about to give up.

Then, on December 4, 1835, a man named Ben Milam arrived. He convinced Burleson to let him take command and attack San Antonio de Bexar. Then he gave a stirring speech to the Texans, drew a line in the sand, and asked those who were willing to go with him to step across it.

Milam's plan was to pretend to attack the Alamo, a walled compound on the other side of the San Antonio River, across from San Antonio de Bexar. Then, when the Mexicans went to defend the Alamo, the Texans would march into San Antonio.

At 5:00 A.M. on December 5, 1835, the Texans fired a cannon at the Alamo. The Mexicans ran to defend it, and the Texans were able to march into San Antonio without any opposition. However, once they were inside San Antonio, the Texans didn't have an easy time. They fought with the Mexicans for four days, much of the time in hand-to-hand combat. There were only 210 Texans against six times as many Mexicans. Also, the Mexicans had the advantage in **artillery**. Nevertheless, the Texans outfought the Mexicans, and on December 9, 1835, the Mexicans surrendered. Only four Texans had been killed during the siege. General Cós and his defeated soldiers were allowed to return to Mexico.

However, Mexican troops soon would return under the leadership of Santa Anna himself.

👆 Actors portraying Alamo defenders re-enact the fall of the Alamo annually to honor the memory of the men who died there. The Alamo is one of the most popular tourist sites in Texas, drawing visitors to San Antonio every year.

SANTA ANNA

THOUGH THINGS WERE GOING WELL FOR THE TEXANS, THAT WASN'T THE CASE IN Zapatecas, the other Mexican province that revolted. The reason was Santa Anna.

When Zapatecas and Texas rebelled, Santa Anna decided to attack Zapatecas first. There were valuable silver mines in Zapatecas that Santa Anna wanted to control.

Zapatecas also had a large militia. However, the militia in Zapatecas was not well trained. Their commander, Francisco Garcia, had no previous military experience. This lack of training and experience would prove devastating for the Zapatecans.

Santa Anna and 4,000 Mexican troops reached Guadalupe, about four miles from Zapatecas, on May 9, 1835. The next morning, after receiving blessings from the priest, about 4,000 Zapatecans marched to Guadalupe. However, they did not attack immediately.

Santa Anna sent a message that they had eight hours to surrender. The Zapatecans refused. That night, May 10, 1835,

David Crockett was born August 17, 1786, in North Carolina. He left home at age 13 to avoid a whipping from his father and traveled about for three years. He returned, married, fought in the war against the Creek Indians, and eventually ended up in Tennessee where he was elected to the legislature.

He became more and more of a character in politics and grew famous. Then, in 1831, a play based on Davy Crockett added to his fame. After a biography about him was published in 1833, Crockett decided to write his autobiography, which made him even more famous. Crockett was a folk hero known throughout the nation. Crockett loved being famous. He liked to boast about his great hunting deeds.

However, when he lost his bid for re-election in the fall of 1835, suddenly he was no longer in the spotlight. He decided he would go to Texas for adventure. As he made his way there, he was greeted as a hero and celebrity wherever he went. He finally made his way to San Antonio de Bexar, just before the siege on the Alamo in February of 1836.

Santa Anna had his soldiers build large bonfires and left a few hundred troops behind to make noise dancing, laughing, and singing. Santa Anna wanted to make the Zapatecans think that his troops would not be attacking that evening.

However, Santa Anna took the main part of his troops and posted them around the Zapatecan campsite. Early the next morning, Santa Anna attacked. The inexperienced Zapatecans were no match for Santa Anna's professional soldiers. After two hours, Santa Anna ordered a ceasefire. About 1,200

In late 1835, volunteer soldiers calling themselves the "Army of the People" assembled to fight for Texas' freedom from Mexico. Although the odds were against the Texans, Mexican troops surrendered San Antonio de Bexar after a five-day battle. This 1845 colored lithograph depicts the fight for San Antonio.

Zapatecans had been killed and 2,723 had been taken prisoner, while Santa Anna had lost only about 100 men. He also had captured all of the Zapatecan artillery and more than 6,000 muskets.

Now the Zapatecans would be punished. Luckily, most of the citizens of Zapateca had left the city. For two days, Santa Anna's soldiers looted Zapatecas. The soldiers raped women,

Davy Crockett was considered an American folk hero in his time. He gained fame as an Indian fighter, pioneer, politician, and freedom fighter, but many people today know of him through the invented accounts of his wild west adventures.

poisoned wells, slaughtered animals, and stole anything worth taking. Everything was destroyed.

There were some Anglos in Zaptecas, and they were special targets of Santa Anna. He ordered that all Anglos were to be killed.

Santa Anna was a big hero in Mexico. When he went to other cities, they gave parades in his honor. His picture was pasted everywhere, and the government in Mexico City named him "Hero of the Fatherland." Santa Anna had destroyed the Zapatecans. Now he would go after the Texans.

Santa Anna took some time to rest, assemble and train his soldiers, and plot his strategy against the Texans. Finally, he and his soldiers began the long march to Texas. Santa Anna crossed the Rio Grande River on February 16, 1836, and by February 21, 1836, he was at Medina.

While Santa Anna destroyed Zapatecas, a lot was happening in Texas, too. The cause of Texas's independence was promoted throughout America. Between October 1835 and April 1836, more than 1,500 persons volunteered to join the Texas army. Many, like Davy Crockett and Jim Bowie, came from outside Texas, looking for adventure, glory, and wealth.

At the same time, Texan leaders couldn't agree on what to do. Some wanted to declare independence and some didn't. Eventually, the governing council dissolved, and two different men claimed to be governor of Texas.

Also, the Texans couldn't decide how to fight. One faction wanted to invade Matamoros instead of waiting for the Mexicans to come to them. Sam Houston, Texas's great military commander, opposed the move.

However, on January 3, 1836, most of the Texan soldiers left San Antonio de Bexar. Houston caught up with them and found three commanders fighting over who would be in charge. Soon, the expedition to Matamoros fell apart, and many of the soldiers went off to fight elsewhere. James Fannin took over as commander of the army, and he led the remaining troops to Goliad.

Unfortunately, the expedition to Matamoros had taken most of the troops, leaving only 104 men to defend San Antonio de Bexar. Captain J. C. Neill, now in charge, decided their best chance if the Mexicans attacked was to fight from inside the Alamo, an old mission compound that had been changed into a military **barracks** by the Spanish army in the early 1800s. The Alamo hadn't been designed to be a real fort, but Neill and his soldiers did the best they could to turn it into one. They dug trenches, mounted cannons, and created barriers.

The Texans' main problem would be their lack of men. They had 19 pieces of artillery, but it took six people to operate each piece. Neill didn't even have enough men to shoot the cannons, much less guard the walls of the Alamo.

Sam Houston thought that there were too few men to defend San Antonio de Bexar, and he sent a recommendation to the governor of Texas, Henry Smith, that the city should be abandoned. He also sent Jim Bowie to San Antonio.

However, when Bowie and the nearly 30 men who rode with him arrived in San Antonio de Bexar, they saw that Neill had turned the Alamo into a fort. Bowie decided to stay. He told the governor that he and Neill had decided to die at the Alamo rather than give it up to the Mexican army.

There were rumors about Santa Anna's army, but no one knew for sure when they would come. Neill appealed to Governor Smith for help. Smith told William Travis to raise up a company of 100 volunteers and take them to San Antonio de Bexar, but he only gave Travis $100 to accomplish this task. Travis was able to muster 26 men, but they were short of food and supplies. Travis and his men arrived at San Antonio on February 3, 1836. A few days later, Davy Crockett and a few men traveling with him arrived at San Antonio also. However, Neill needed a lot more men.

Captain Neill received news that his family was ill, so on February 11, 1836, he left San Antonio de Bexar to take care of them. He left William Travis in charge. However, many of the volunteers didn't want to serve under Travis. They preferred to be commanded by Jim Bowie. The command ended up being divided, with Bowie leading the volunteers and Travis leading the regular soldiers.

Some of the volunteers were *Tejanos* (Hispanic Texans) under the command of Juan Seguin. These men had families who lived on the land that Santa Anna would cross to reach San Antonio de Bexar. Some asked for permission to leave the Alamo to go protect their families, and about a dozen left on February 21, 1836. No one knew exactly where Santa Anna was; they had no way of knowing he would arrive in just two more days.

with all dispatch — The enemy is receiving reinforcements daily & will no doubt increase to three or four thousand in four or five days. If this call is neglected, I am determined to sustain myself as long as possible & die like a soldier who never forgets what is due to his own honor & that of his country —

Victory or Death

William Barret Travis
Lt. Col. comdt.

P.S. The Lord is on our side — When the enemy appeared in sight we had not three bushels of corn — We have since found in deserted houses 80 or 90 bushels & got into the walls 20 or 30 head of Beeves —

Travis

🕯 Shortly before the fall of the Alamo, William Travis wrote a letter, asking for reinforcements to help defend the fort. Unfortunately, few men were able to make it to the Alamo in time. Travis signed the letter "Victory or Death;" a bold prophecy.

TRAPPED AT THE ALAMO

and sounds of a jubilant **fiesta**. Both *Tejanos* and Anglos, soldiers and citizens, danced, drank, and ate until the early morning hours of February 23.

However, when they woke up that day, the Texans saw that people were leaving San Antonio de Bexar very quickly. The *Tejanos* had heard what the Anglos soon found out—Santa Anna and his soldiers were only a few miles away.

Travis ordered his men to join Bowie's inside the Alamo. The Texans had not expected Santa Anna so soon, and therefore they had not stored up food and supplies. Now they took what food they could find from the shacks of poor *Tejanos*.

Travis had only about 150 men. Even worse, Jim Bowie had become ill. Travis sent messages to the Texan commanders at Gonzales and Goliad, begging them to send troops to help him.

That afternoon, Santa Anna and about 1,500 troops marched into San Antonio de Bexar. A military band played while the Texans waited inside the Alamo.

Texas has a nickname—the Lone Star State. The state flag has a single star. There are many stories about when and how the flag came to be. The present version of the flag was officially adopted in 1839. Texas did not become a state until 1845, so for several years Texas was an independent republic.

Santa Anna removed the Texans' flag from the plaza and hoisted a blood red flag with a skull and crossbones in the center of it. Santa Anna was letting the defenders in the Alamo know he would show them no more mercy than he had Zapatecas. The Texans hoisted a white flag, indicating they wanted to talk. However, Jim Bowie and William Travis each acted separately.

Bowie sent a note with a messenger. The Mexicans sent back a reply that only unconditional surrender would be permitted, although the response mentioned the possibility of **clemency**. However, given the cruelty Santa Anna had shown the Zapatecans, he might have killed the Texans even if they had surrendered unconditionally.

Meanwhile, Travis sent a man named Albert Martin to speak with a colonel in Santa Anna's army. Travis offered to surrender if he and his men could leave. This is what the Texans had done for the Mexican army when they'd captured General Cós and his army at this same spot only a couple of months before. However, the Mexicans said that only unconditional surrender would be permitted. This the Texans would not do.

Less than 24 hours earlier, the Texans had been partying in

👆 Only 26 years old, William Travis had difficulty commanding the respect of his men. At the Alamo he was in charge of the regular soldiers, while Jim Bowie commanded the volunteers.

San Antonio, dancing and drinking. Now Travis's voice was serious as he spoke to his men inside the Alamo. He told them they were fighting for Texas, for freedom, and for their lives.

The next day, Travis sent a famous letter addressed to "the People of Texas & all Americans in the world." After explaining that the Mexicans had demanded unconditional surrender and promised they would kill everyone if the

The single star in Texas's state flag is a reminder of Texas's short history as an independent republic.

Texans refused, Travis concluded:

> I have answered the demand with a cannon shot, & our flag still waves proudly from the walls. I shall never surrender or retreat.
>
> I call on you in the name of Liberty, of patriotism & every thing dear to the American character, to come to our aid with all dispatch…If this call is neglected, I am determined to sustain myself as long as possible & die like a soldier who never forgets what is due his own honor & that of his country.

He ended his letter "VICTORY or DEATH." Only if additional Texans came to San Antonio de Bexar would the men at the Alamo have a chance. Travis hoped his passionate letter would inspire others to help the men trapped at the Alamo.

The Mexicans shelled the Alamo during the next few days and nights, but they didn't try to seize it. Santa Anna had more

William Barrett Travis was born on August 1, 1809, in South Carolina. His family soon moved to Alabama, where Travis grew up. He received a good education and after briefly working as a teacher, took up the study of law. He also started a newspaper when he was only 19 years old. He married, quickly had children, and found himself getting deeper and deeper in debt. Creditors began to sue him, and his marriage was unhappy. To avoid going to jail for his debts, Travis left his wife and children and went to Texas in April of 1831.

There is also another story about why Travis left Alabama for Texas. He is said to have murdered a man he thought was having an affair with his wife. Supposedly, he was assigned to defend another man that was charged with the very same murder. When the jury convicted this man, Travis secretly revealed his guilt to the judge, who advised him to run to Texas.

There, he set up a law practice, learned to speak Spanish, and gained the respect of Texan citizens, some of whom nicknamed him "Buck." He also got involved in the Texas Independence movement. He began to buy land in Texas.

Travis met a woman in Texas he wanted to marry, so in 1835 he and his wife in Alabama agreed to divorce. Travis' son was brought to Texas to be raised by Travis. However, Travis enlisted in the volunteer army of Texas in September of 1835 and he never had the chance to raise his son.

troops on the way to San Antonio. He also was expecting much larger cannons that could literally knock down the Alamo's walls.

On February 25, 1836, Santa Anna sent a couple of **battalions** to try to get a position closer to the Alamo. The

Juan Seguin was a member of an important Tejano family—his father had been *alcalde*, or mayor, of San Antonio. Seguin was born in 1806. By the time he was 28 years old, in 1834, he was involved in San Antonio politics.

Seguin was critical of the harsh policies of Mexico's president, Santa Anna. In 1835, he recruited a force of Mexican ranchers in Texas and led them against the Mexican army. He fought in the first battle at the Alamo in December 1835. Because of his bravery, he won a commission as a captain in the Texas army.

When William Travis arrived at the Alamo on February 3, 1836, Seguin was among the 26 men with him. However, he left the Alamo on February 25, when the fort was surrounded by Santa Anna's men. Because Seguin spoke both Spanish and English, he was told to take Travis's letter requesting reinforcements through the enemy lines to Gonzales, 70 miles away. Seguin was returning to the Alamo when it fell on March 6.

After distinguishing himself at the battle of San Jacinto, Seguin became governor of San Antonio and held a burial service for the Alamo dead. Though he had served Texas well, in 1842 he was forced to leave the country and return to Mexico. But Seguin longed to live in Texas, and he returned there in 1848.

Texans fired at the Mexicans, and the Mexicans had to back off. However, Travis knew that this hadn't been a full attack and that the Texans were in trouble. The Mexicans were surrounding them, setting up **batteries** all around. That night, the Mexicans tried another assault at a different part of the fort. However, they were only testing the Texans' defenses.

The men inside the Alamo dug trenches and fortified walls. They slipped out and burned down some shacks near the Alamo, so that the Mexican soldiers would have nothing to hide behind. Travis knew, though, that soon the Mexicans would attack with all of their forces. He had received no response to his request for reinforcements, and now he decided to send someone important to plead with the Texas commander at Goliad to send help.

James Fannin, the commander at Goliad, had problems of his own. While Santa Anna was attacking the Alamo, another Mexican general, Jose Urrea, probably the best general in the Mexican army, was headed toward Goliad. Fannin himself had been begging for more help, but he decided he could not ignore Travis's request.

On February 26, 1836, Fannin left 100 of his men at Goliad and started marching the other 300 toward the Alamo. However, when they ran into a few difficulties on the first day (a wagon broke down, some oxen wandered off), Fannin decided to turn back. He learned a couple of days later that Urrea was only 50 miles away and had defeated a group of Texans; Fannin decided that sending help to the Alamo wasn't possible.

On the night of February 25, Travis had sent another message, desperately asking for help. He sent this one to Gonzales, 70 miles away. "It will be impossible for us to keep them out much longer," Travis wrote. "If they overpower us, we fall a sacrifice at the shrine of our country, and we hope posterity and our country will do our memory justice. Give us help, oh my Country!"

The messenger was Juan Seguin, a prominent *Tejano* from San Antonio who had joined the Texans' cause. Seguin was chosen because he could speak both English and Spanish and had the best chance of getting past the soldiers surrounding the fort. Seguin left the fort at night, bluffed his way past a Mexican patrol, and raced for Gonzales. Once there, Seguin tried to raise a force of *Tejanos* to come back with him to the Alamo. However, there would not be time.

But Travis's letter had stirred the hearts of Texans. Governor Smith called upon fellow Texans to come to the aid of those at the Alamo. Even as far away as New Orleans, people were declaring that help was needed.

Yet no one came. And some were leaving. During a pause in the fighting on February 29, 1836, some of the *Tejanos* still inside the Alamo had second thoughts about staying, especially when their leader, Seguin, wasn't there. Bowie told them they could do as they wished. Most of them left.

Inside the fort, the Texans worked hard to shore up the fortifications, so they could withstand the Mexican attack. The constant bombardment by Santa Anna's army had been nerve-wracking. Though the cannons pounded the walls, the Alamo remained strong.

Early on the morning of February 30, the Texans heard voices outside the Alamo. Shots were fired, but then someone told the

Texans to hold their fire. Then 32 volunteers from Gonzales rode into the Alamo. They had managed to sneak past the Mexicans. However, except for two or three more men, no more help would arrive at the Alamo. And soon, the Mexicans would attack.

Davy Crockett, out of ammunition, swings his rifle in a futile defense against thousands of Mexican soldiers. There are conflicting stories about Crockett's death. Some historians believe he was cut down while defending the Alamo, while other sources have claimed that he surrendered but was executed on the orders of Santa Anna.

5

SLAUGHTER AND MORE SLAUGHTER

MEANWHILE, ON FEBRUARY 28, 1836, TEXANS WERE MEETING IN WASHINGTON-ON-THE-BRAZOS TO draft a constitution and declare independence. Though Texan armies were losing to Mexican armies at the time, Texans were determined to be independent.

At the same time, Texas politicians were questioning the letter that Travis had sent asking for help. Some claimed that Travis was creating a crisis simply to make himself more important. They said the danger wasn't as great as Travis said. Others said the letters were forgeries. Even the great Sam Houston thought Travis and Fannin were exaggerating. Unfortunately, many dismissed Travis's plea for help.

The men in the Alamo knew none of this. And they were encouraged by some good news. Colonel James Butler Bonham and two other Texans made it through the Mexican lines in broad daylight and joined the men at the Alamo. Bonham brought with him a letter from R.M. Williamson that said Texans were rushing to the Alamo. It promised that 60 men were coming from Gonzales, 300 from Goliad, and maybe

Texas Independence was declared on March 2, 1836. Texans still celebrate March 2 as Texas Independence Day.

another 300 from other towns in Texas. Williamson begged Travis to hold out until help arrived.

However, the message was wrong. No more men were coming. Travis suspected that the promise of help would not prove true.

And if things weren't bad enough already, more troops arrived for Santa Anna on March 3. The Mexicans now had about 2,500 troops—more than 10 Mexicans for every Texan.

Santa Anna and his officers met the afternoon of March 4, 1836, to discuss whether to wait or attack now. If they waited for the big cannons, they could simply blow down the walls of the Alamo. On the other hand, if help for the Texans was headed to the Alamo, waiting could allow the Texans to gain the advantage. After hearing his officers' opinions, Santa Anna said he would make a decision the next day.

On the evening of March 4, 1836, some Mexican women left the Alamo and went to Santa Anna. They told him how few Texans were inside the Alamo. Santa Anna decided he would attack immediately.

There are many legends about the Alamo. One is that on March 5, 1836, William Travis made a speech to his men. In that speech, Travis supposedly told his men they were going

The battle at the Alamo was a bloody, chaotic, and confusing fight. It took more than 600 Mexican soldiers to defeat the 183 defenders of the Alamo, partly due to "friendly fire," meaning the Mexicans accidentally shot some of their own men.

👆 Davy Crockett was famed for his crack shooting, and his signature weapon was his long rifle, "Old Betsy." The rifle was presented to him as a gift, and the inscription on the barrel reads: "Go Ahead."

to die. There was no way to avoid it. But they had a choice about how they wanted to die:

They could surrender to the Mexicans and be executed.

They could try to run and get shot escaping.

They could stand and fight inside the Alamo until they could fight no more and were killed.

These were the choices. Then, Travis drew his sword and with it drew a line in the sand. He said whoever was willing to stay and die with him in the Alamo should step across the line. All but one man did so; a soldier named Louis Rose fled into the night and was never heard from again. Jim Bowie was too sick to get up and had to be carried over the line. No one knows for sure if events really happened this way, but it is one of the most famous stories about the Alamo.

Santa Anna met with his officers the afternoon of March 5

to plan their assault. At midnight on March 6, 1836, they woke the Mexican soldiers and started moving them into position. At some time between 5 and 5:30 A.M., the bugles blew, announcing that it was time to attack. Their military band played as the Mexicans charged.

How and where Jim Bowie and Davy Crockett died is not clear. Most accounts say that Bowie died in his sick bed, either before the Mexicans found him or fighting off the Mexicans from his deathbed. How Davy Crockett died also is controversial. Some stories say he died in battle but other accounts say he was captured and then executed along with five other Texans.

The Texans took their positions, but they couldn't see much—the sun had not yet risen. Even though the Mexicans were within range of the Texans' Kentucky long rifles, the Texans could only see a distance of a few yards.

William Travis was one of the first to be shot when he was hit in the head with a bullet. According to his servant, a slave named Joe, even after he was hit he was able to run his sword through a Mexican general who was trying to cut his head off.

The assault turned into mass confusion. With the poor visibility and Mexicans coming from many directions, the Mexicans ended up shooting more of their own soldiers than they shot Texans. Twenty minutes into the attack, the Mexicans managed to breach the north wall of the Alamo, and the Texans ran there to fight them off. At the south wall, Davy Crockett and

The Kentucky long rifle, also called the Pennsylvania long rifle, was one of the most accurate guns of the time. The barrel was more than three and a half feet long and was "rifled" with spiral grooves inside. The length of the barrel and the rifling made the gun more accurate than other guns; it was accurate up to 200 yards.

his men were fighting off another attack. Then the Mexicans managed to make their way over the west wall. Mexicans were now coming into the Alamo from the west and the north.

The Mexicans captured an 18-pound cannon inside the Alamo and turned it on the Texans. For about an hour, Mexicans and Texans fought hand to hand. Texans hiding in rooms poked a white flag through holes as if they were going to surrender, then shot and stabbed Mexicans as they came in.

But the Mexicans showed no mercy either. They killed the sick, along with a few Texans that tried to escape. They spared only a few women and children and the slave, Joe.

After an hour or two, the battle was over. Between 700 to 800 people lay dead, more than 500 of them Mexican. Mexican soldiers mutilated and stripped the Texan corpses.

Two important sources we have about what happened at the Alamo are Susanna Dickerson, whose husband was killed in the battle, and Joe, the servant of William Travis. Joe identified the bodies of Travis and Bowie for Santa Anna. Santa Anna took Susanna and her daughter prisoner. He offered to send them to Mexico City, but she begged to be released. Santa Anna agreed and told her to go to Gonzales and tell everyone how strong and ruthless he was. She and Joe arrived in Gonzales on March 20, 1836.

Sam Houston had already arrived there on March 11. He had heard about what happened at the Alamo and feared the same thing would happen at Goliad. He sent a message to James Fannin, advising him to leave immediately. However Fannin delayed until the morning of March 19 and retreated slowly.

Mexican General Urrea arrived on the same day, shortly after Fannin left. He quickly caught up with Fannin near Coleto Creek early on the afternoon of March 11, 1836. Although the woods nearby offered cover, Fannin decided to stand and fight out in the open. This was a terrible decision.

The next day, Fannin raised a white flag, indicating he would surrender. Urrea sent a message to Santa Anna, asking that the lives of Fannin and his troops be spared, but Santa Anna replied that all of them were to be slaughtered.

And they were. On Palm Sunday, March 27, 342 Texans were executed by the Mexicans. They even executed the sick and wounded. Like at the Alamo, the Texans were not buried. Their bodies were burned.

Even though the men at the Alamo were defeated, their failure raised support for the cause of Texas. Suddenly, everyone in America cared about Texas. The slaughters at the Alamo and at Goliad needed to be avenged.

The Texans avenged the Alamo defeat just six weeks later with their victory at the battle of San Jacinto. This painting depicts Santa Anna (in a green jacket and white pants) being presented to Sam Houston (reclining under the tree).

VICTORY AT SAN JACINTO

THE FATE OF TEXAS'S INDEPENDENCE WOULD REST IN THE HANDS OF SAM HOUSTON. AT FIRST, many Texans feared that he wasn't up to the job. However, Houston wasn't afraid—he was smart.

When the news of what happened at the Alamo reached Sam Houston, he decided to retreat with his soldiers to the Colorado River. The soldiers were not happy with his decision, nor were the people in Gonzales. They wanted revenge, but Sam Houston wanted victory. He wanted to fight the Mexicans at a time and place where Texas, not Mexico, would win.

Soon, news of the massacre at Goliad reached Houston's ears. Again, Houston decided to retreat, back to the Brazos River. Many criticized Houston, thinking he was cowardly. After all, Houston had far more troops than those who had bravely died at the Alamo. Soon Houston would retreat even further, this time to Mill Creek.

Houston knew his troops were not properly trained. He ignored his critics and focused on turning his undisciplined volunteers into a real army. Soon Houston would have his chance.

The Texas government had moved to Harrisburg. Santa Anna decided to take 950 men to go after them. Houston heard about Santa Anna's plan and marched his own men there, arriving on April 18, 1836. This, he had decided, was the time and place to take on the Mexicans.

Houston gave a rousing speech to his men on April 19, 1836. He told them, "Remember the Alamo!" His troops began to shout, "Remember the Alamo! Remember Goliad!"

Santa Anna was nearby with about 800 soldiers. Houston decided to attack before more Mexican troops arrived.

By the evening of April 20, 1836, the Texans and Mexicans were camped only a thousand yards from each other. Houston knew that Mexican reinforcements were near, and unfortunately, they arrived the next morning. General Cós and his men increased the Mexican army to more than 1,200 men, more than Houston's 900.

Houston told his men to burn Vince's Bridge. This would prevent any more Mexicans from coming to help Santa Anna. However, it also meant that if the Texans did not win, they would not be able to escape.

On April 21, 1836, Houston made his move. The Mexicans were not expecting an attack in broad daylight, and they were completely surprised. As they charged, the Texans shouted, "Remember the Alamo!" and "Remember Goliad!"

The battle turned into a **rout** for the Texans. The battle was over in less than 20 minutes, but the Texans were anxious for revenge; they continued killing Mexicans even after they'd

 Sam Houston was a leader in the Texas War for Independence. His tactics before and during the battle of San Jacinto helped Texas secure its freedom form Mexico.

won the battle. Houston tried to stop them, but his men paid him no attention. They remembered what Santa Anna had done to Texans at the Alamo and at Goliad.

Only nine Texans died during the battle, compared with more than 650 Mexicans. An additional 500 Mexicans were taken prisoner. One of these prisoners was Santa Anna.

A song called "The Yellow Rose of Texas" was written by an unknown Texan soldier after the battle at San Jacinto. This

The largest city in Texas today is named after Sam Houston, a leader in the War for Texas Independence. Houston was born in Tennessee in 1793, the son of a major in the U.S. Army. He studied to become a lawyer, but when the War of 1812 broke out he joined the army and served with distinction. After the war, Houston completed his law studies. He was elected to Congress in 1823, and in 1827 became governor of Tennessee.

Houston was not as successful in his personal life as in his public life. He was devastated when his marriage ended. He left his position as governor and went to live in the mountains of Tennessee with the Cherokee Indians. Some scholars believe he may have taken a Cherokee wife during this time; it is certain that he had a drinking problem. By 1833 he had left the United States altogether and headed to Texas.

Houston soon found himself involved in Texas politics. In 1836 he was placed in charge of the Texas Army. His leadership, especially in the battle of San Jacinto, resulted in victory for Texas in the war for independence.

Houston served twice as president of the Republic of Texas. After Texas was admitted to the United States as a state in 1845, Houston continued to hold political office. He served as a U.S. Senator from 1846 to 1859, when he was elected governor. However, Houston opposed Texas secession from the Union—an issue which 76 percent of his state supported. When Texas voted to join the Confederate States of America in the spring of 1861, Houston sadly resigned his position. For the last two years of his life, he watched the state he had helped to create and wondered what would happen to it after the Civil War. Sam Houston died on July 25, 1863.

song, well known today, is based on a legend about why Santa Anna was unprepared when the Texans attacked at San Jacinto. It is said that on the day of the battle at San Jacinto, Santa Anna was distracted by a beautiful woman named Emily Morgan. Emily was a slave or servant girl he had chosen to entertain him that afternoon. This is supposed to be the reason that the Mexicans were unprepared for the attack by the Texans.

Santa Anna had changed from his uniform into civilian clothes to disguise his identity during the battle at San Jacinto. However, he had neglected to remove the diamond studs from his silk shirt, and his captured troops shouted "El Presidente" when they saw them. This gave away his identity.

In fact, there was an Emily D. West, a free woman, who was probably captured by the Mexicans during a raid at Galveston a few days before the battle at San Jacinto. If she really was with Santa Anna on the day the Texans attacked, she probably was not there willingly. However, the idea that the "Yellow Rose of Texas" distracted Santa Anna so that the Texans could win the battle of San Jacinto is a famous legend in Texas history.

Though Santa Anna had been ruthless to the Texans, now that he was a prisoner, he begged for mercy. He claimed that the slaughter of helpless prisoners at Goliad and the Alamo had happened only because the Mexican government had ordered it, ignoring the fact that he was the head of the Mexican government.

Sam Houston was not interested in revenge; he was more interested in making peace with Mexico and securing the independence of Texas. He agreed to spare Santa Anna's life in exchange for a treaty. Santa Anna promised that Mexico would never fight with Texas again. He and the new president of Texas, David G. Burnet, signed the treaty. Santa Anna was allowed to leave, alive.

Santa Anna returned to Mexico, where he eventually regained power. Although he had agreed to recognize Texas's independence, he never really did, and skirmishing continued for the next decade. But the liberty of Texas was never in doubt after the battle of San Jacinto.

In September 1836, Texans voted for the constitution that had been drawn up the previous March at Washington-on-the-Brazos. The government of the new independent republic was similar to that of the United States: it had a president, a two-house congress, and a supreme court. Sam Houston was elected president by a wide margin; he received more than 5,000 votes, nearly 10 times as many as Stephen Austin.

With Mexico now unable to control immigration into the region, the population of Texas quickly grew. Newcomers to the republic received a huge grant of free land—between 320 and 1,280 acres, depending on when they arrived. This helped the population increase from about 35,000 in 1836 to 140,000 by 1847, and to more than 600,000 by 1860. Texas's days as an independent republic ended in 1845, when it was admitted to the United States as a state.

The battle of the Alamo played a key role in the war for Texas's independence. In military terms, the fight was not very significant—the garrison at the Alamo was too small to have much of an impact on the army of Texas. In psychological terms, however, the impact was tremendous. The story of the gallant defenders of the Alamo quickly spread through Texas, the United States, and the rest of the world. The Alamo showed that for the Texans, there were no alternatives. They would either win their freedom or die in the attempt. Santa Anna's brutal slaughter of the Alamo defenders also inspired a deep anger and a desire for revenge in the Texans—a revenge they earned six weeks later at the battle of San Jacinto.

GLOSSARY

Artillery

Weapons for discharging missiles.

Barracks

Buildings used for lodging soldiers.

Battalions

Groups of troops organized to act together.

Batteries

Units of troops in the army that are armed with artillery.

Cavalry

Troops mounted on horseback.

Civil rights

Rights that all citizens of a society are supposed to have.

Clemency

An instance of showing mercy or leniency.

Commerce

Buying and selling, or doing business.

Conquistador

Spanish conqueror.

Conservative

Unwilling to change rapidly.

Constitution

The written laws and basic principles of a nation or social group, determining the powers and duties of the government and guaranteeing certain rights to the people.

Factions

Groups that disagree with each other.

Fiesta

The Spanish word for "party"; a celebration.

Militias

Groups of citizens organized for military service.

Rout

A disastrous defeat.

Siege

A persistent and serious attack.

Skirmishes

A minor fight in a larger war.

TIMELINE

1822
Stephen F. Austin brings a group of American settlers to Texas

1833
Stephen Austin goes to Mexico City to ask that Texas be permitted to form its own state government. He is arrested by Antonio López de Santa Anna and thrown in jail for 18 months.

1834
Santa Anna overthrows Mexican government, does away with Mexico's constitution, and becomes dictator.

1835
On March 30, the Mexican province of Zapatecas rebels against Santa Anna. Santa Anna crushes the Zapatecas rebellion and slaughters the Zapatecans May 10-12.

In July, Stephen Austin is released from Mexican prison.

On October 1, citizens in Gonzales, Texas, refuse Mexican orders to surrender a cannon. Instead, they fire on Mexican troops, starting the War for Texas Independence. Nine days later, on October 10, a group of Texas volunteers capture Mexican soldiers at Gonzales. The next day, Stephen Austin is elected commander.

From December 5 to 9, Texas volunteers fight 1,200 Mexican soldiers and take control of San Antonio de Bexar and the Alamo.

1836
On January 3, most of the Texas volunteers leave San Antonio de Bexar for an expedition to Matamoros. Only about 100 volunteers remain to guard San Antonio de Bexar and the Alamo. Captain Neill and his men work to make the Alamo a better fort. Later in the month, Jim Bowie and about thirty men arrive at the Alamo to help Captain Neill.

In response to Neill's request for men to defend the Alamo, on February 3 William Travis arrives with about 26 men. A few days later, Davey Crockett arrives with a few men. Captain Neill leaves San Antonio to care for his sick family on February 11. He leaves Travis in charge, but the camp soon splits up into two groups—one that wants to follow Bowie and another that wants to follow Travis. Travis and Bowie agree to share the command. However, in a few days Bowie becomes so sick that he is unable to lead.

A dozen of the Tejanos who belong to the Texas volunteers leave San Antonio on February 21. Two days later, after a festival, the volunteers at the Alamo awake to see that many residents of San Antonio are quickly leaving because Santa Anna and his army have been seen only a few miles away. All the volunteers enter the Alamo. 1,500 Mexican troops march into San Antonio. Santa Anna hoists a blood-red flag, letting the Texans know that he will show them no mercy.

From February 23 to 29, the Mexican army shells the Alamo. Although there are some minor skirmishes, Santa Anna does not yet launch a full attack on the Alamo. Travis continues to hope for more help. By February 29, most of the Tejanos have left the Alamo.

Texas declares independence on March 2. The next day, more Mexican troops arrive at the Alamo. Santa Anna has more than 10 times as many troops as there are Texans defending the old mission.

On March 6, Santa Anna attacks the Alamo at dawn. The battle is quickly over. The 183 Texan defenders of the Alamo either die in battle or are executed by the Mexicans. On March 11–12, Mexican general José Francisco Urrea captures the Texan volunteers trying to escape from Goliad. After they surrender, Santa Anna orders them all executed.

On April 21, Sam Houston attacks the Mexicans at San Jacinto. The Texans score a major victory and capture Santa Anna. Days later, Santa Anna agrees to a peace treaty with Texas that essentially grants its freedom.

1845

On December 29, U.S. president James K. Polk signs the Texas Admission Act, making Texas a part of the United States.

FURTHER READING

Davis, William C. *Three Roads to the Alamo*. New York: Harper Collins, 1998.

Fisher, Leonard Everett. *The Alamo*. New York: Holiday House, 1987

Garland, Sherry. *Voices of the Alamo*. New York: Scholastic Press, 2000

Harmon, Daniel E. *Davy Crockett*. Philadelphia: Chelsea House Publishers, 2002.

Jakes, John. *Susanna of the Alamo, a True Story.* San Diego: Harcourt Brace Jovanovich, 1986.

Long, Jeff. *Duel of the Eagles: The Mexican and U.S. Fight for the Alamo.* New York: Quill, 1990.

Marcovitz, Hal. *The Alamo*. Philadelphia: Mason Crest Publishers, 2003.

Matovina, Timothy M. *The Alamo Remembered: Tejano Accounts and Perspectives*. Austin: University of Texas Press, 1995.

Roberts, Rand and Olson, James S. *A Line in the Sand: The Alamo in Blood and Memory*. New York: The Free Press, 2001.

Tinkle, Lon. *Thirteen Days to Glory: The Seige of the Alamo*. Austin: Texas A&M University Press, 1985.

Wade, Linda R. *Alamo: Battle of Honor and Freedom*. New York: Rourke, 1991.

INTERNET RESOURCES

The battle of the Alamo
http://www.americanwest.com/pages/alamo.html
http://www.thehistorynet.com/WildWest/articles/ 02962_text.html
http://www.lsjunction.com/events/alamo.html
www.kwanah.com/txmilmus/tnghist3.htm

Information on Davy Crockett, William Travis, Jim Bowie, Sam Houston, and Santa Anna
http://www.americanwest.com/pages/davycroc.htm
http://www.lsjunction.com/people/travis.htm
http://www.lsjunction.com/people/bowie.htm
http://www.shsu.edu/pin_www/HouSerL.html
http://www.lsjunction.com/people/santanna.htm

Daughters of the Republic of Texas
http://www.drtl.org

Goliad
http://www.tpwd.state.tx.us/park/goliad/goliad.htm

The Alamo
http://www.thealamo.org/

INDEX

PHOTO CREDITS

ABOUT THE AUTHOR

Mike Wilson has published articles on history in magazines for children. He also has written instructional material for Harcourt Brace and will have a biography of Father Roy Bourgois published by John Gordon Burke Publishers.